Mein erstes Lernbuch
ENGLISCH
Grundschule

Lernen und Nachschlagen

Von Birgit Fuchs
Illustriert von Manfred Tophoven

Tessloff Verlag

Foreword
Vorwort

Herzlich willkommen in deinem **Ersten Lernbuch Englisch Grundschule** und in der Welt von Billy Malone!
Auf den nächsten Seiten lernst du Billy und seine Familie kennen und entdeckst, wie die Familie Malone lebt. Gleichzeitig lernst du viele wichtige und nützliche englische Wörter und übst deine ersten englischen Sätze.

Und so kannst du mit diesem Lernbuch üben:
In den **Bildern** auf jeder Seite findest du Beschriftungen vieler Gegenstände in Englisch und Deutsch. So kannst du dir die Vokabeln zu den einzelnen Themen leicht einprägen. In den **Randspalten** findest du noch mehr Bilder und Vokabeln, die deinen Wortschatz ergänzen können. **Billy's basics** beinhalten einfache englische Grammatik für einen allerersten Überblick. Und schließlich erfährst du unter der Rubrik **Make sentences**, wie du mit den Wörtern, die du gelernt hast, deine ersten englischen Sätze bilden kannst.

Am besten lernst du Englisch, wenn du so viel wie möglich sprichst! Lass dir die englischen Wörter von jemandem vorlesen, der Englisch kann, damit du dir gleich die richtige Aussprache einprägst.

Damit man genau weiß, wie die Wörter ausgesprochen werden, gibt es die so genannte **Lautschrift.** Sie benutzt bestimmte Zeichen, die immer für einen ganz bestimmten Laut stehen. Im Vokabelverzeichnis am Ende des Lernbuchs findest du hinter jedem englischen Wort auch die dazugehörige Lautschrift.

Dies sind die wichtigsten Zeichen:

ɑː	wie in lahm	aɪ	wie in Mai	v	wie in Vase
iː	wie in Biene	ɔɪ	wie in Eule	z	wie in Sonne
uː	wie in Blume	aʊ	wie in Haus	s	wie in Messer
i	wie in Baby	eə	ähnlich wie in leer		Diese Laute gibt es nur in Englisch:
ɪ	wie in Kiste	ɪə	wie in Tier		
e	wie in Bett	ɜː	ähnlich wie in hört	θ	wie in think
æ	wie in Bär	dʒ	wie in Dschungel	ð	wie in this
ʌ	wie in Kamm	ʒ	wie in Garage	w	wie in water
ɒ	wie in Motte	ŋ	wie in Ring	r	wie in red
ə	wie in Mitte	ʃ	wie in Schlange	eɪ	wie in day
ʊ	wie in Butter	tʃ	wie in tschüss	əʊ	wie in low

Contents
Inhalt

Numbers from 1 to 100	Zahlen von 1 bis 100	4
The Malones, Billy's family	Die Malones, Billys Familie	6
The Malones' house	Das Haus der Malones	8
In the garden	Im Garten	10
In the living room	Im Wohnzimmer	12
In the kitchen	In der Küche	14
In the children's room	Im Kinderzimmer	16
In the bathroom	Im Badezimmer	18
My body	Mein Körper	20
Clothes	Kleidung	22
At school	In der Schule	24
Animals	Tiere	26
On the farm	Auf dem Bauernhof	28
Food	Lebensmittel	30
In town	In der Stadt	32
Opposites	Gegensätze	34
What is Billy doing?	Was macht Billy gerade?	36
At the fair	Auf dem Jahrmarkt	38
The Malones are very busy	Die Malones sind sehr beschäftigt	40
At the swimming pool	Im Schwimmbad	42
Sport	Sport	44
At the campsite	Auf dem Zeltplatz	46
At the doctor's	Beim Arzt	48
Professions	Berufe	50
The weather	Das Wetter	52
The year and the seasons	Das Jahr und die Jahreszeiten	54
Vocabulary	Vokabeln	56

Numbers from 1 to 100
Zahlen von 1 bis 100

1  one	2 two	3 three	4 four	5 five
11 eleven	12 twelve	13 thirteen	14 fourteen	15 fifteen
21 twenty-one	22 twenty-two	23 twenty-three	24 twenty-four	25 twenty-five
31 thirty-one	32 thirty-two	33 thirty-three	34 thirty-four	35 thirty-five
41 forty-one	42 forty-two	43 forty-three	44 forty-four	45 forty-five
51 fifty-one	52 fifty-two	53 fifty-three	54 fifty-four	55 fifty-five
61 sixty- one	62 sixty-two	63 sixty-three	64 sixty-four	65 sixty-five
71 seventy-one	72 seventy-two	73 seventy-three	74 seventy-four	75 seventy-five
81 eighty-one	82 eighty-two	83 eighty-three 	84 eighty-four	85 eighty-five
91 ninety-one	92 ninety-two	93 ninety-three	94 ninety-four	95 ninety-five

6 six	7 seven	8 eight	9 nine	10 ten
16 sixteen	17 seventeen	18 eighteen	19 nineteen	20 twenty
26 twenty-six	27 twenty-seven	28 twenty-eight	29 twenty-nine	30 thirty
36 thirty-six	37 thirty-seven	38 thirty-eight	39 thirty-nine	40 forty
46 forty-six	47 forty-seven	48 forty-eight	49 forty-nine	50 fifty
56 fifty-six	57 fifty-seven	58 fifty-eight	59 fifty-nine	60 sixty
66 sixty-six	67 sixty-seven	68 sixty-eight	69 sixty-nine	70 seventy
76 seventy-six	77 seventy-seven	78 seventy-eight	79 seventy-nine	80 eighty
86 eighty-six	87 eighty-seven	88 eighty-eight	89 eighty-nine	90 ninety
96 ninety-six	97 ninety-seven	98 ninety-eight	99 ninety-nine	100 a hundred

The Malones, Billy's family
Die Malones, Billys Familie

Mary, Billy's mother
Mary, Billys Mutter und

Laura, Billy's grandmother
Laura, Billys Großmutter

Susan, Billy's baby sister
Susan, Billys kleine Schwester

Peter, Billy's father
Peter, Billys Vater

Joe, Billy's grandfather
Joe, Billys Großvater

Tom, Billy's uncle
Tom, Billys Onkel

Claire, Billy's aunt
Claire, Billys Tante

Peggy, Billy's cousin
Peggy, Billys Cousine

Charly, Billy's dog
Charly, Billys Hund

Billy

Sally, Billy's sister
Sally, Billys Schwester

Ron, Billy's cousin
Ron, Billys Cousin

Billy's basics

I	– ich	I am (I'm)	– ich bin
you	– du	you are (you're)	– du bist
he, she, it	– er, sie, es	he, she, it is (he's, she's, it's)	– er, sie, es ist
we	– wir	we are (we're)	– wir sind
you	– ihr	you are (you're)	– ihr seid
they	– sie	they are (they're)	– sie sind

parents — Eltern
adults — Erwachsene

woman — Frau
wife — Ehefrau

man — Mann
husband — Ehemann

boy — Junge
son — Sohn
brother — Bruder

girl — Mädchen
daughter — Tochter
sister — Schwester

child — Kind
children — Kinder

Make sentences!

I'm Billy. I'm Sally's brother.
Ich bin Billy. Ich bin Sallys Bruder.

I'm Mary. I'm Peter's wife.
Ich bin Mary. Ich bin Peters Frau.

This is Mary. She is Billy's mother.
Das ist Mary. Sie ist Billys Mutter.

I'm Sally. I'm Mary's daughter.
Ich bin Sally. Ich bin Marys Tochter.

The Malones' house
Das Haus der Malones

book
Buch

ball
Ball

watering can
Gießkanne

helicopter
Hubschrauber

tree
Baum

tree Baum
bird Vogel
balloon Ballon
gutter Dachrinne
window Fenster
garage Garage
hedge Hecke
car Auto
flowers Blumen

Billy's basics

on	– auf	in front of	– vor
under	– unter	between	– zwischen
behind	– hinter	next to	– neben
over	– über		

8

bird	Vogel
balloon	Ballon
letter box	Briefkasten
hammer	Hammer
flower	Blume
cat	Katze

Labels on the picture:
- chimney — Schornstein
- roof — Dach
- helicopter — Hubschrauber
- cat — Katze
- lamp — Lampe
- door — Tür
- balcony — Balkon
- letter box — Briefkasten
- house — Haus
- bench — Bank
- stairs — Treppe
- hammer — Hammer
- lawn — Rasen
- doll — Puppe

Make sentences!

Where is the balloon? — The balloon is over the garage.
Wo ist der Ballon? — Der Ballon ist über der Garage.

Where is the book? — The book is on the bench.
Wo ist das Buch? — Das Buch ist auf der Bank.

In the garden
Im Garten

leaf — Blatt
grass — Gras
sun — Sonne
sunflower — Sonnenblume
rose — Rose

bush — Busch
slide — Rutsche
rose — Rose
spade — Schaufel
bucket — Eimer
sand — Sand
ball — Ball
spider's web — Spinnenetz
spider — Spinne
worm — Wurm

Billy's basics

I can see	– ich kann sehen	we can see	– wir können sehen
you can see	– du kannst sehen	you can see	– ihr könnt sehen
he, she, it can see	– er, sie, es kann sehen	they can see	– sie können sehen

a (an) – ein, eine   the – der, die, das

tree Baum
fence Zaun
sunflowers Sonnenblumen
squirrel Eichhörnchen
seesaw Wippe
sandpit Sandkasten
stone Stein
pond Teich
duck Ente
ladybird Marienkäfer
fish Fische

bee Biene
butterfly Schmetterling
fly Fliege
ant Ameise
spider Spinne
beetle Käfer

Make sentences!

I can see the sun.
Ich kann die Sonne sehen.

I can see the grass.
Ich kann das Gras sehen.

I can see a butterfly.
Ich kann einen Schmetterling sehen.

I can see an ant.
Ich kann eine Ameise sehen.

In the living room
Im Wohnzimmer

candle	Kerze
vase	Vase
newspaper	Zeitung
magazine	Zeitschrift
budgie	Wellensittich

Labels in picture: books / Bücher, cage / Käfig, budgie / Wellensittich, candle / Kerze, clock / Uhr, CDs / CDs, plant / Pflanze, cupboard / Schrank, playpen / Laufstall, armchair / Sessel, blanket / Decke

Billy's basics

I am looking for	– ich suche	we are looking for	– wir suchen
you are looking for	– du suchst	you are looking for	– ihr sucht
he, she, it is looking for	– er, sie, es sucht	they are looking for	– sie suchen

picture — Bild
lamp — Lampe
bookshelf — Bücherregal
television — Fernseher
CD player — CD-Spieler
sofa — Sofa
telephone — Telefon
carpet — Teppich
magazine — Zeitschrift
cushion — Kissen

telephone — Telefon
cushion — Kissen
remote control — Fernbedienung
mobile phone — Handy
blanket — Decke
plant — Pflanze

Make sentences!

Billy is looking for the book.
Billy sucht das Buch.

Sally is looking for the magazine.
Sally sucht die Zeitschrift.

In the kitchen
In der Küche

pot — Topf
cup — Tasse
plate — Teller
glass — Glas
knife — Messer

fruit — Obst
clock — Uhr
cupboard — Schrank
toaster — Toaster
microwave — Mikrowelle
dustpan — Kehrblech
broom — Besen
chair — Stuhl
fridge — Kühlschrank

Billy's basics

Look, there is … – Schau, da ist / da gibt es …
Look, there are … – Schau, da sind …

- dishes — Geschirr
- oven cloth — Topflappen
- coffee machine — Kaffeemaschine
- cooker — Herd
- oven — Backofen
- dishwasher — Spülmaschine
- sink — Spüle
- tap — Wasserhahn
- ironing board — Bügelbrett
- iron — Bügeleisen
- dustbin — Mülleimer
- dishcloth — Geschirrtuch
- table — Tisch

- saucer — Untertasse
- fork — Gabel
- spoon — Löffel
- bowl — Schüssel
- pan — Pfanne
- bottle — Flasche

Make sentences!

Look, there is a plate on the table!
Schau, da ist ein Teller auf dem Tisch!

Look, there are cups in the cupboard!
Schau, da sind Tassen im Schrank!

In the children's room
Im Kinderzimmer

football — Fußball
umbrella — Regenschirm
teddy bear — Teddybär
doll — Puppe

teddy bear — Teddybär
picture — Bild
calendar — Kalender
wardrobe — Kleiderschrank
mirror — Spiegel
pillow — Kopfkissen
bed — Bett
drawer — Schublade
puppet theatre — Puppentheater
ladder — Leiter
glove puppet — Handpuppe
doll — Puppe

Billy's basics

I have got	– ich habe	I (ich)	– my (mein)
you have got	– du hast	you (du)	– your (dein)
he, she, it has got	– er, sie, es hat	he, she, it (er, sie, es)	– his, her, its (sein, ihr, sein)
we have got	– wir haben	we (wir)	– our (unser)
you have got	– ihr habt	you (ihr)	– your (euer)
they have got	– sie haben	they (sie)	– their (ihr)

clock — Uhr
blind — Rollo
poster — Poster
window — Fenster
radio — Radio
windowsill — Fensterbank
computer — Computer
toys — Spielzeug
scissors — Schere
chair — Bürostuhl
desk — Schreibtisch
picture book — Bilderbuch

toy car — Spielzeugauto
clock — Uhr
skipping rope — Hüpfseil
pencil — Bleistift
glove puppet — Handpuppe

Make sentences!

I've got a dog. It's my dog.
Ich habe einen Hund. Es ist mein Hund.

We've got a picture book.
Wir haben ein Bilderbuch.

It's our picture book.
Es ist unser Bilderbuch.

She's got a ball. It's her ball.
Sie hat einen Ball. Es ist ihr Ball.

They've got a computer.
Sie haben einen Computer.

It's their computer.
Es ist ihr Computer.

In the bathroom
Im Badezimmer

soap — Seife
comb — Kamm
hairbrush — Haarbürste
toothbrush — Zahnbürste
toothpaste — Zahncreme

door — Tür
shower curtain — Duschvorhang
towels — Handtücher
bathrobe — Bademantel
shower gel — Duschgel
radiator — Heizung
shower — Dusche
cupboard — Schrank
clothes — Kleidung
shoes — Schuhe
bath mat — Badematte

Billy's basics

red	– rot	black	– schwarz
blue	– blau	grey	– grau
green	– grün	purple	– lila
yellow	– gelb	orange	– orange
pink	– rosa	brown	– braun

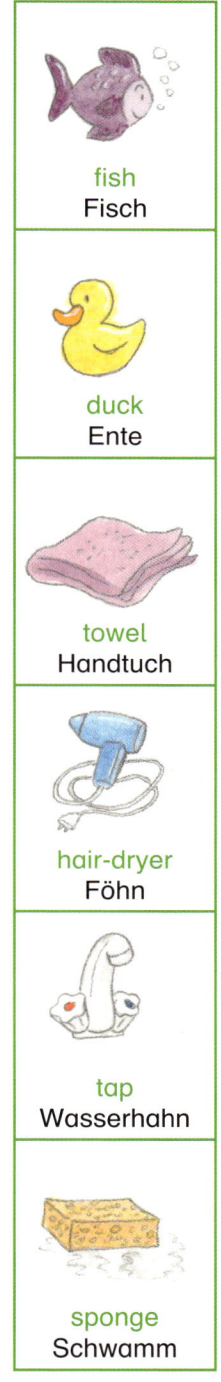

tiles	Fliesen
mirror	Spiegel
socket	Steckdose
flush	Spülung
tap	Wasserhahn
rubbish bin	Mülleimer
toilet paper	Toilettenpapier
basin	Waschbecken
toilet	Toilette
bath	Badewanne
rubber duck	Gummiente
fish	Fisch
duck	Ente
towel	Handtuch
hair-dryer	Föhn
tap	Wasserhahn
sponge	Schwamm

Make sentences!

What colour is the soap? The soap is green.
Welche Farbe hat die Seife? Die Seife ist grün.

What colour is the towel? The towel is pink.
Welche Farbe hat das Handtuch? Das Handtuch ist rosa.

My body
Mein Körper

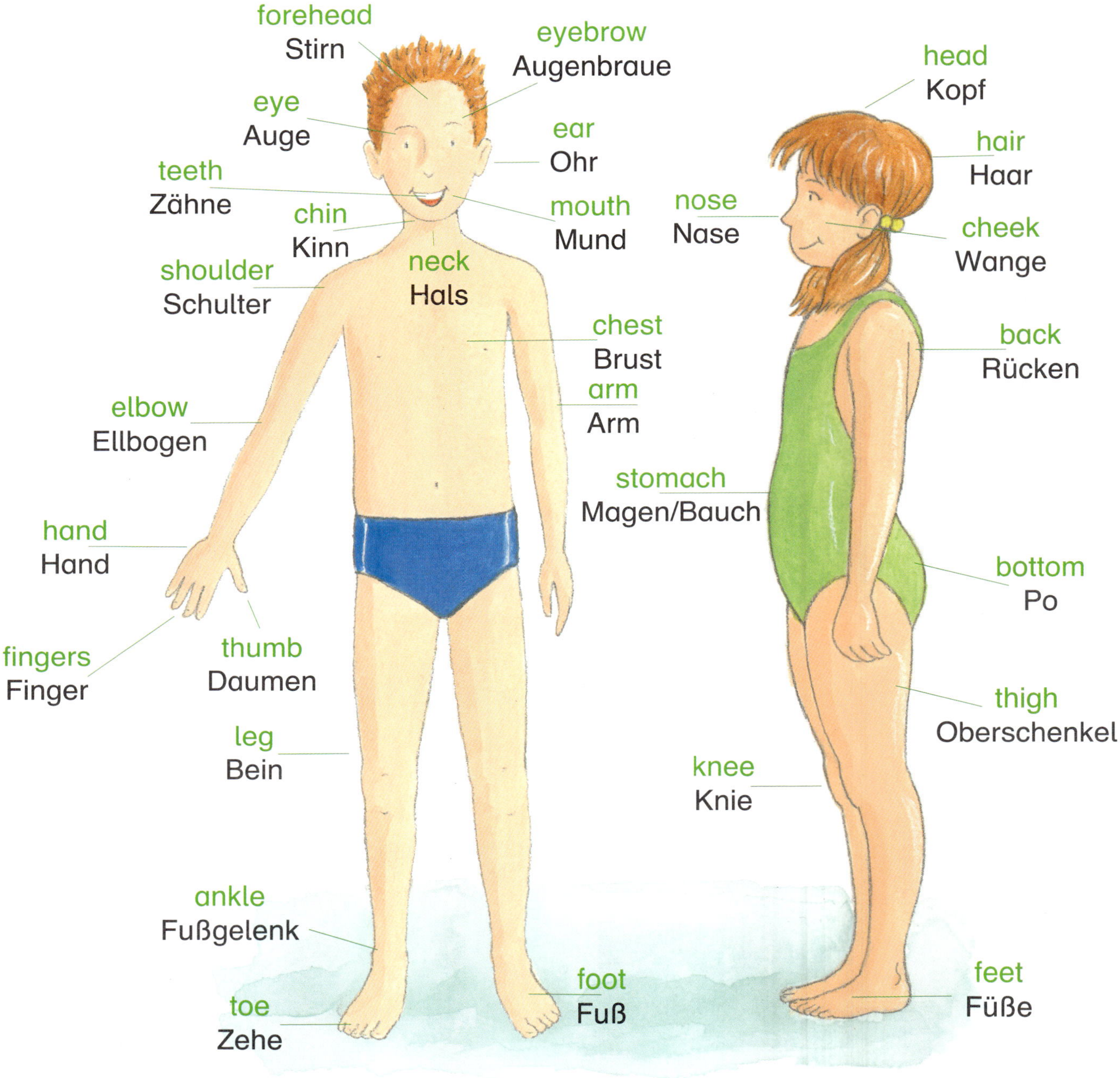

forehead	Stirn
eyebrow	Augenbraue
head	Kopf
eye	Auge
ear	Ohr
hair	Haar
teeth	Zähne
nose	Nase
chin	Kinn
mouth	Mund
cheek	Wange
shoulder	Schulter
neck	Hals
chest	Brust
back	Rücken
arm	Arm
elbow	Ellbogen
stomach	Magen/Bauch
hand	Hand
bottom	Po
fingers	Finger
thumb	Daumen
leg	Bein
thigh	Oberschenkel
knee	Knie
ankle	Fußgelenk
toe	Zehe
foot	Fuß
feet	Füße

Billy's basics

It is called…	– Es wird…genannt.
This part is called…	– Dieser Teil wird…genannt.
This part of the body…	– Dieser Teil des Körper…

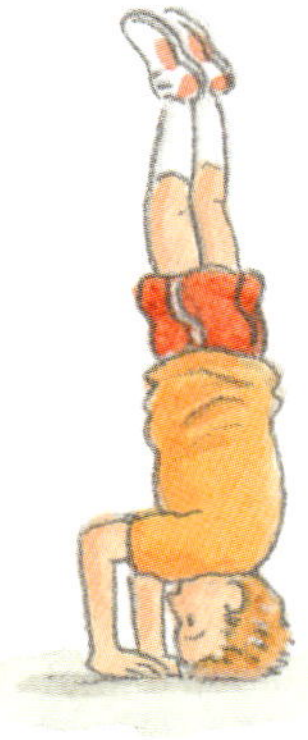

cartwheel
Rad

knee bend
Kniebeuge

headstand
Kopfstand

handstand
Handstand

back bend
Brücke

one-leg stand
Waage

forward roll
Rolle vorwärts

backward roll
Rolle rückwärts

Make sentences!

This part of the body is called the knee.
Dieser Teil des Körpers wird Knie genannt.

I can do a headstand.
Ich kann einen Kopfstand machen.

Clothes
Kleidung

- **jumper** — Pullover
- **cap** — Mütze
- **tie** — Krawatte
- **hat** — Hut
- **gloves** — Handschuhe
- **cap** — Kappe
- **vest** — Unterhemd
- **T-shirt** — T-Shirt
- **pyjamas** — Schlafanzug
- **pants** — Unterhose
- **suit** — Anzug
- **trousers** — Hose
- **shorts** — Shorts
- **trainers** — Turnschuhe
- **rucksack** — Rucksack
- **boots** — Stiefel
- **shoes** — Schuhe
- **swimming trunks** — Badehose
- **slippers** — Hausschuhe

Billy's basics

it is (it's)	– es ist …
it is not (it isn't)	– es ist nicht … / es ist kein …
this is	– dies ist …
this isn't	– das ist nicht … / das ist kein …
these are	– dies sind …
these aren't	– das sind nicht … / das sind keine …

scarf — Schal
mittens — Fäustlinge
jacket — Jacke
raincoat — Regenmantel
swimsuit — Badeanzug
coat — Mantel
bag — Tasche
nightdress — Nachthemd
jeans — Jeans
dress — Kleid
socks — Socken
cardigan — Strickjacke
tights — Strumpfhose
sandals — Sandalen
wellington boots — Gummistiefel
bikini — Bikini
belt — Gürtel
skirt — Rock
blouse — Bluse

Make sentences!

It's a dress. It isn't a skirt.
Es ist ein Kleid. Es ist kein Rock.
This is a skirt. This isn't a bag.
Das ist ein Rock. Das ist keine Tasche.

At school
In der Schule

chalk
Kreide

sponge
Schwamm

exercise book
Heft

pencil sharpener
Anspitzer

pen
Füller

TIME	MONDAY	TUESDAY	WEDNESDAY	THURSDAY	FRIDAY
9.00	Maths Mathe	English Englisch	Maths Mathe	English Englisch	General Studies Sachkunde
9.50	Reading Lesen	Reading Lesen	PE Sport	Reading Lesen	English Englisch
10.30	Break Pause	Break Pause	Break Pause	Break Pause	Break Pause
10.50	Music Musik	Maths Mathe	English Englisch	German Deutsch	Maths Mathe
11.40	English Englisch	French Französisch	English Englisch	Religious Education Religion	Maths Mathe
12.20	Lunch Mittagessen	Lunch Mittagessen	Lunch Mittagessen	Lunch Mittagessen	Lunch Mittagessen
1.00	Science Naturwissenschaft	General Studies Sachkunde	Art Kunst	Science Naturwissenschaft	Reading Lesen
2.00	Physical Education Sport	Religious Education Religion	Reading Lesen	Maths Mathe	Science Naturwissenschaft
3.00	HOME	HOME	HOME	HOME	HOME

chalk
Kreide

timetable
Stundenplan

sponge
Schwamm

Billy's basics

1. first   – der / die / das Erste; erstens
2. second   – der / die / das Zweite; zweitens
3. third   – der / die / das Dritte; drittens
4. fourth   – der / die / das Vierte; viertens
5. fifth   – der / die / das Fünfte; fünftens
6. sixth   – der / die / das Sechste; sechstens

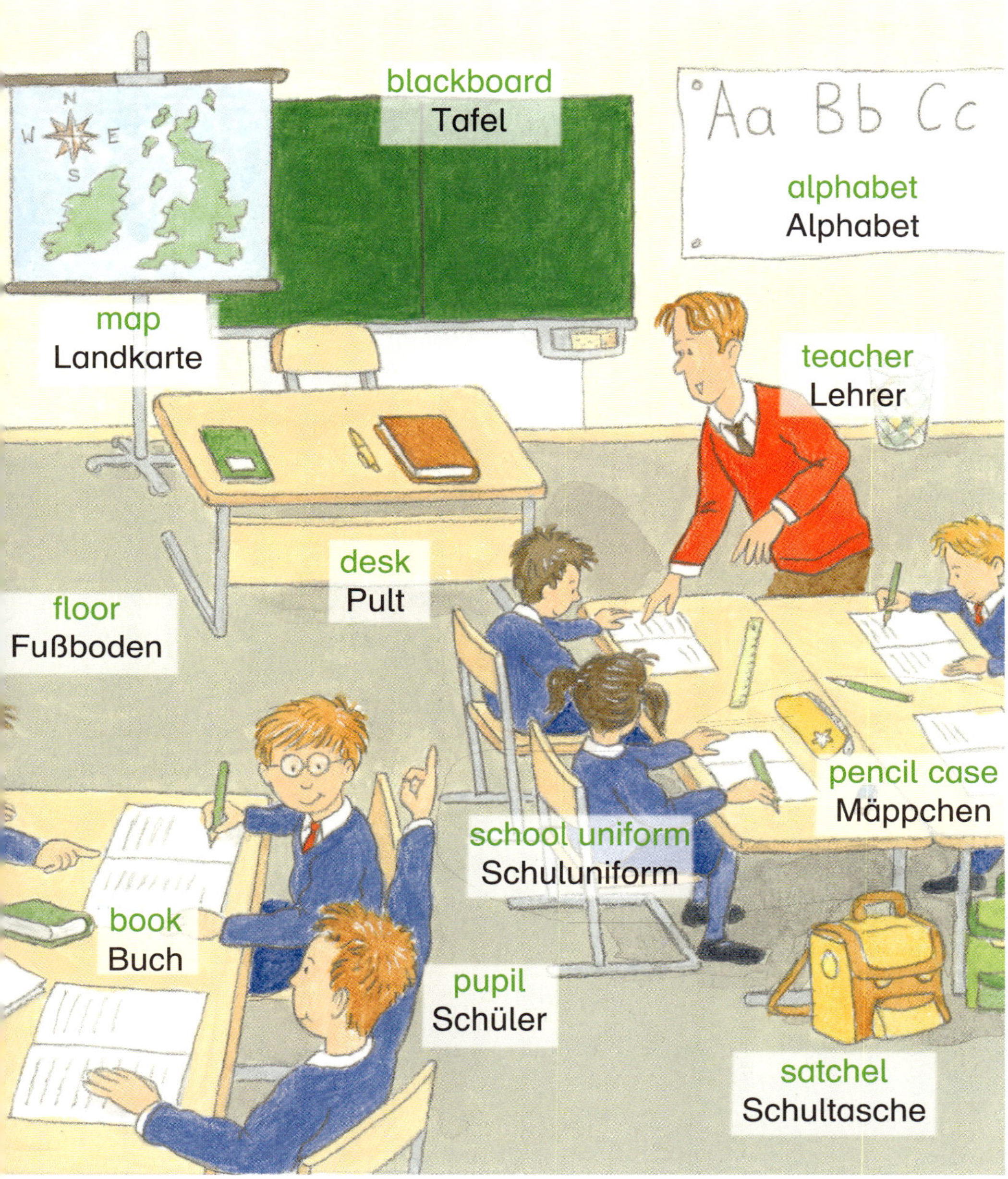

pencil
Bleistift

ruler
Lineal

rubber
Radiergummi

biro
Kugelschreiber

paper
Papier

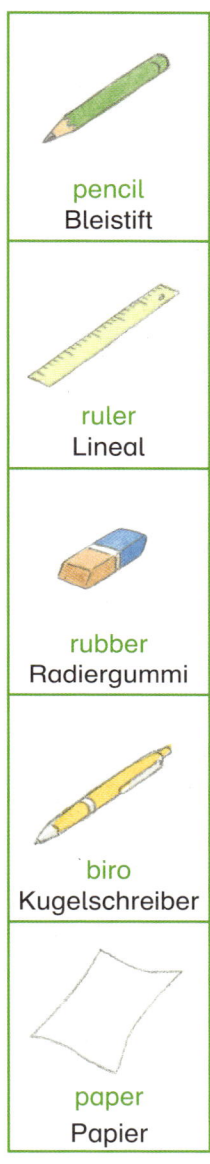

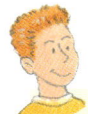

Make sentences!

On Monday we've got six lessons.
Am Montag haben wir sechs Unterrichtsstunden.

The first lesson is maths.
Die erste Unterrichtsstunde ist Mathe.

Animals
Tiere

dolphin Delfin	**peacock** Pfau	**flamingo** Flamingo	**tiger** Tiger
fox Fuchs		**duck** Ente	**budgie** Wellensittich
guinea pig Meerschweinchen	**rhino** Nashorn		**fish** Fisch
hippo Flusspferd			**crocodile** Krokodil
		snake Schlange	
hamster Hamster	**turtle** Schildkröte	**penguin** Pinguin	**rabbit** Kaninchen	**zebra** Zebra

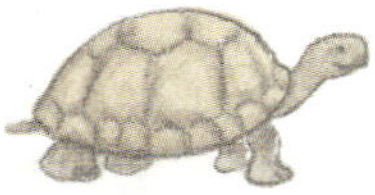

Billy's basics

Do you know ... ?   – Weißt du ...? / Kennst du ...?

bear / Bär	hedgehog / Igel	mouse / Maus	wolf / Wolf		giraffe / Giraffe
dog / Hund	parrot / Papagei		elephant / Elefant		
beaver / Biber	polar bear / Eisbär				
	bird / Vogel			eagle / Adler	
hare / Hase	cat / Katze	monkey / Affe	lion / Löwe		kangaroo / Känguru

Make sentences!

Do you know what this animal is called?
Weißt du, wie dieses Tier heißt?

This is a bear.
Das ist ein Bär.

On the farm
Auf dem Bauernhof

pig — Schwein
goat — Ziege
sheep — Schaf
hen — Henne
cock — Hahn

farmhouse — Bauernhaus
apple tree — Apfelbaum
roof — Dach
ivy — Efeu
bench — Bank
gate — Tor
farmer's wife — Bäuerin
kennel — Hundehütte
dog bowl — Hundenapf
dunghill — Misthaufen
henhouse — Hühnerstall
sheep — Schafe
wheelbarrow — Schubkarre
fence — Zaun

Billy's basics

how many — wie viele
How many things can you see? — Wie viele Dinge kannst du sehen?

horse	Pferd
chick	Küken
duck	Ente
cow	Kuh
dog	Hund
farmer	Bauer

- combine harvester — Mähdrescher
- brick — Ziegelstein
- straw — Stroh
- field — Feld
- barn — Scheune
- pasture — Weide
- wheel — Rad
- hay — Heu
- stable — Stall
- farmer — Bauer
- tractor — Traktor
- pitchfork — Mistgabel
- farm — Hof

Make sentences!

How many cows can you see?   I can see two cows.
Wie viele Kühe kannst du sehen?   Ich kann zwei Kühe sehen.

Food
Lebensmittel

peach	Pfirsich
tomato	Tomate
grapes	Weintrauben
apple	Apfel
honey	Honig

orange — Apfelsine
peach — Pfirsich
pineapple — Ananas
tomato — Tomate
lettuce — Salat
strawberries — Erdbeeren
cucumber — Gurke
cauliflower — Blumenkohl
apple — Apfel
potatoes — Kartoffeln
grapes — Weintrauben
banana — Banane
peas — Erbsen
beans — Bohnen
cherries — Kirschen
plums — Pflaumen
sweetcorn — Mais
mushrooms — Pilze
pear — Birne
lemon — Zitrone
red pepper — roter Paprika
carrot — Möhre

Billy's basics

Can I have ..., please? — Kann ich bitte ... haben?
Thank you. — Danke.
Yes, you can. Here you are. — Ja, hier bitte.
You're welcome. — Bitte schön.

cake	Kuchen
biscuits	Kekse
milk	Milch
lemonade	Limonade
chewing gum	Kaugummi
chocolate	Schokolade
vinegar	Essig
oil	Öl
tea	Tee
eggs	Eier
orange juice	Orangensaft
coffee	Kaffee
cocoa	Kakao
jam	Marmelade
bread	Brot
butter	Butter
cheese	Käse
ham	Schinken
salt	Salz
pepper	Pfeffer
sugar	Zucker
sausages	Würstchen
honey	Honig
sausages	Würstchen
chips	Pommes frites
chewing gum	Kaugummi
lemonade	Limonade
chocolate	Schokolade

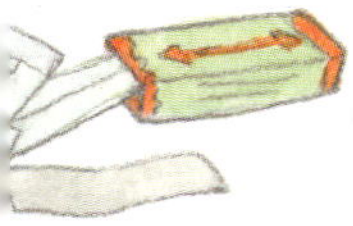

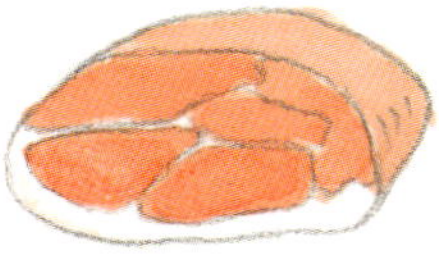

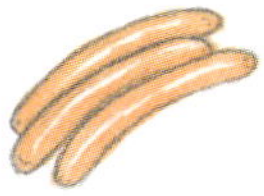

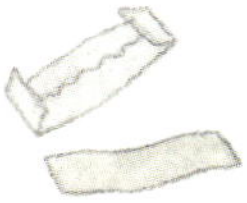

Make sentences!

Can I have a banana, please?
Kann ich bitte eine Banane haben?
Can I have some milk, please?
Kann ich bitte etwas Milch haben?

Yes, you can. Here you are.
Ja, bitte schön.
Thank you. You're welcome.
Danke. Bitte schön.

In town

In der Stadt

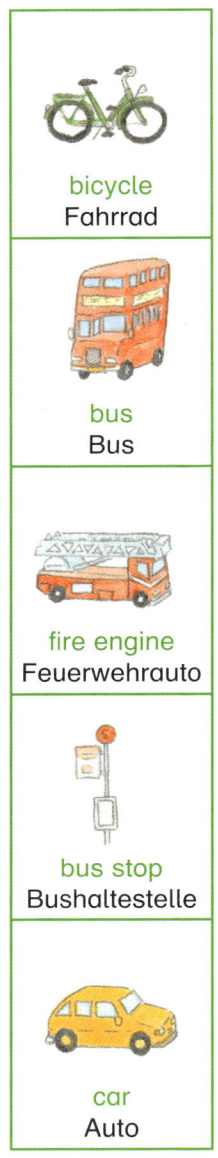

bicycle
Fahrrad

bus
Bus

fire engine
Feuerwehrauto

bus stop
Bushaltestelle

car
Auto

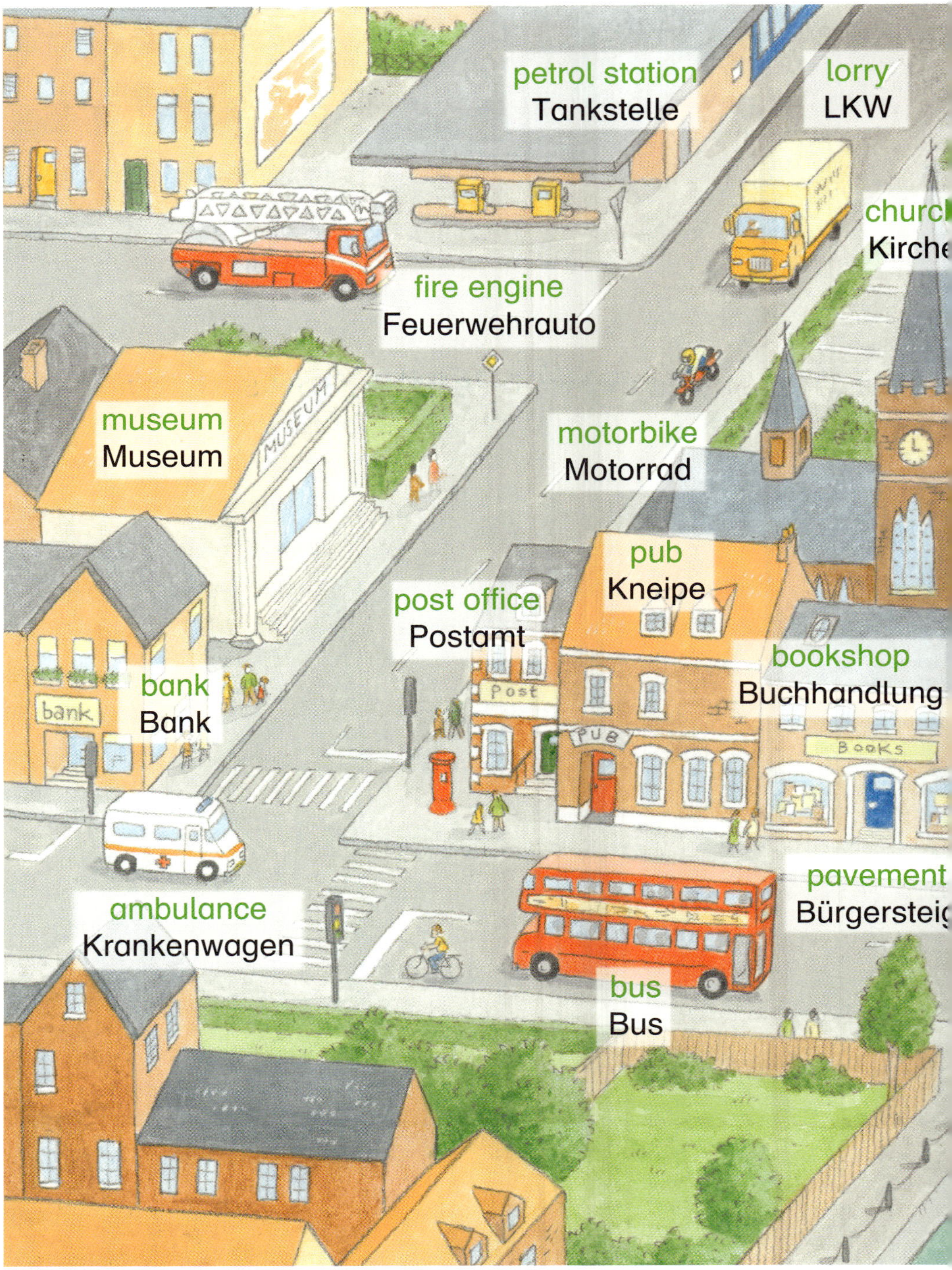
petrol station
Tankstelle
lorry
LKW
churc
Kirch
fire engine
Feuerwehrauto
museum
Museum
MUSEUM
motorbike
Motorrad
pub
Kneipe
post office
Postamt
bookshop
Buchhandlung
bank
Bank
bank
Post
PUB
BOOKS
pavement
Bürgerstei
ambulance
Krankenwagen
bus
Bus

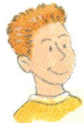

Billy's basics

on the left – links   on the right – rechts

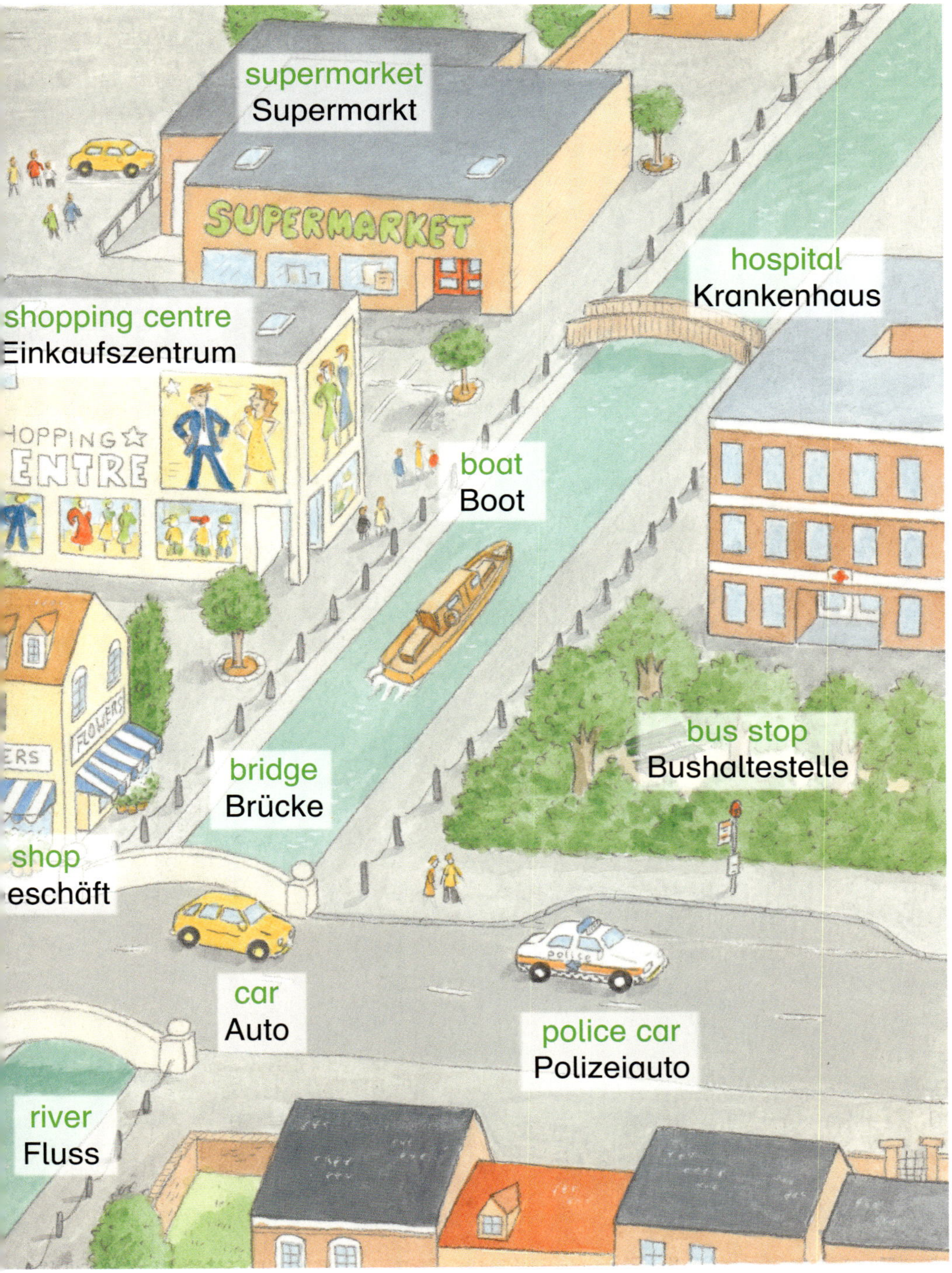

ambulance
Krankenwagen

traffic lights
Ampel

motorbike
Motorrad

lorry
LKW

traffic sign
Verkehrsschild

police car
Polizeiauto

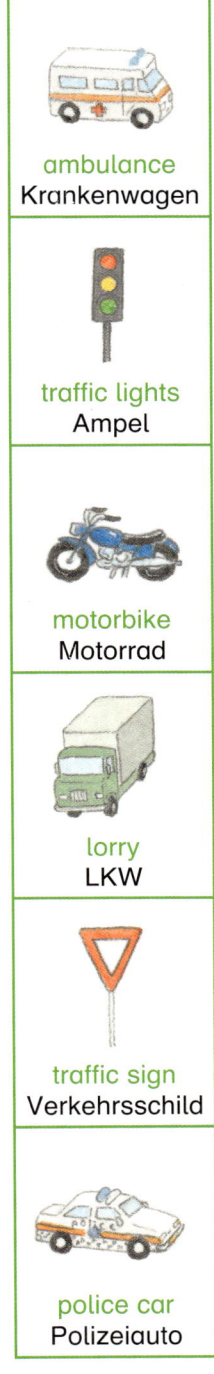

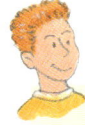

Make sentences!

On the left you can see a church.
Links kannst du eine Kirche sehen.

On the right there is a park.
Rechts ist ein Park.

Opposites
Gegensätze

elephant	Elefant	big groß	fat	dick	cat Katze	dog	Hund	thin dünn	grandfather	Großvater	old alt

grandchild — Enkelkind
young — jung

mouse — Maus
small — klein

bottle — Flasche
glass — Glas
full — voll
empty — leer

snake — Schlange
long — lang

worm — Wurm
short — kurz

coffee — Kaffee 
ice cream — Eis  
hot — heiß
cold — kalt
turtle — Schildkröte
slow — langsam
car — Auto
fast — schnell

Billy's basics

but — aber
the opposite of — das Gegenteil von

Susan — happy / glücklich
Sally — sad / traurig

closed / geschlossen — door / Tür — open / geöffnet
window / Fenster

Susan  — loud / laut
Billy — quiet / leise

butterfly / Schmetterling — beautiful / schön
toad / Kröte — ugly / hässlich

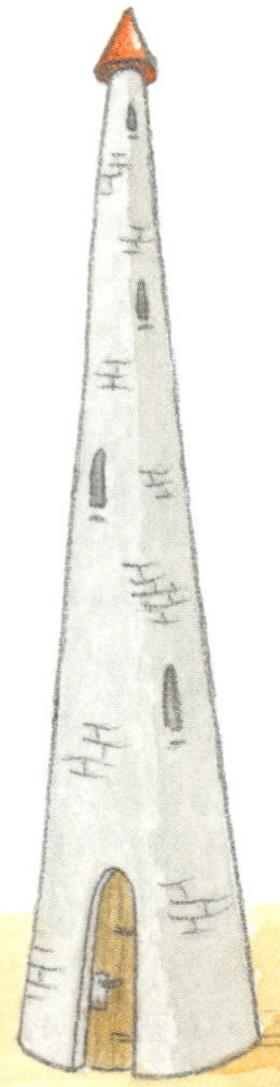

tower / Turm — high / hoch
house / Haus — low / niedrig
stone / Stein — hard / hart
feather / Feder — soft / weich

Make sentences!

The cat is fat, but Charly is thin.　　The opposite of fat is thin.
Die Katze ist dick, aber Charly ist dünn.　Das Gegenteil von dick ist dünn.

What is Billy doing?
Was macht Billy gerade?

to smile
lächeln

to whisper
flüstern

to write
schreiben

to sleep
schlafen

to sing
singen

to dream
träumen

to eat
essen

to run
rennen

to cry
weinen

to wait
warten

to jump
springen

to read
lesen

to kiss
küssen

to drink
trinken

to talk
reden

to swing
schaukeln

Billy's basics

to sing	– singen	we are singing	– wir singen gerade
I am singing	– ich singe gerade	you are singing	– ihr singt gerade
you are singing	– du singst gerade	they are singing	– sie singen gerade
he, she, it is singing	– er, sie, es, singt gerade		

to paint	to clean	to think	to push
malen	putzen	denken	drücken
to climb	to pull	to sit	to draw
klettern	ziehen	sitzen	zeichnen
to walk	to give	to take	to knock
gehen	geben	nehmen	klopfen
to listen	to show	to carry	to shout
zuhören	zeigen	tragen	rufen

Make sentences!

Billy is laughing.
Billy lacht gerade.
Billy is running.
Billy rennt gerade.

Billy is painting
Billy malt gerade.
Billy is waiting
Billy wartet gerade.

37

At the fair
Auf dem Jahrmarkt

balloon
Ballon

ticket
Los

ticket
Eintrittskarte

plastic flower
Plastikblume

candy floss
Zuckerwatte

big wheel
Riesenrad

2£

dragon
Drachen

3£

1£

1£

clown
Clown

bumper car
Autoskooter

Billy's basics

How much is ...? – Wie viel kostet ...?
How much are ...? – Wie viel kosten ...?

38

roller coaster
Achterbahn

ghost train
Geisterbahn

3£

2£

roundabout
Karussell

1£   1£   1£

1£   1£

2£
1£
2£
1£

chips
Pommes frites

hot dog
Hotdog

hamburger
Hamburger

ice cream
Eis

popcorn
Popcorn

Coke
Cola

Make sentences!

How much is a ticket for the roller coaster?   It costs .... pounds.
Was kostet eine Karte für die Achterbahn?   Sie kostet ... Pfund.

The Malones are very busy
Die Malones sind sehr beschäftigt

to wake up
aufwachen

to wash the car
das Auto waschen

to play football
Fußball spielen

to do homework
Hausaufgaben machen

Billy's basics

six o'clock	– sechs Uhr (6.00 Uhr)
half past nine	– halb zehn (9.30 Uhr)
quarter past seven	– Viertel nach sieben (7.15 Uhr)
quarter to one	– Viertel vor eins (12.45 Uhr)
a.m.	– morgens (0.00 bis 12.00)
p.m.	– abends (12.00 bis 0.00)

to go for a walk
spazieren gehen

to go shopping
einkaufen gehen

to bake a cake
einen Kuchen backen

to watch television
fernsehen

Make sentences!

At six o'clock Susan wakes up.
Um sechs Uhr wacht Susan auf.
At half past four Billy plays football.
Um halb fünf spielt Billy Fußball.

At the swimming pool
Im Schwimmbad

life belt
Rettungsring

beach ball
Wasserball

diving rings
Tauchringe

water wings
Schwimmflügel

lilo
Luftmatratze

Dusche — shower
Sauna — sauna
Fußbad — footbath
beach ball — Wasserball
to swim — schwimmen
starting block — Startblock
solarium — Solarium
diving rings — Tauchringe
rubber ring — Schwimmring

Billy's basics

Let's go to … . – Lass uns zum … gehen.
Let's play with … . – Lass uns mit … spielen.

Temperatur
temperature
24°

Bademeister
bath superintendent

loudspeaker
Lautsprecher

plant
Pflanze

life belt
Rettungsring

diving board
Sprungbrett

to dive
tauchen

water
Wasser

water wings
Schwimmflügel

water slide
Wasserrutsche

towel
Handtuch

lilo
Luftmatratze

sun lounger
Sonnenliege

rubber ring	Schwimmring
water slide	Wasserrutsche
sun lounger	Sonnenliege
diving board	Sprungbrett
starting block	Startblock
pool	Becken

Make sentences!

Let's go to the pool!
Lass uns zum Schwimmbecken gehen!

Let's play with the diving-rings!
Lass uns mit den Tauchringen spielen!

43

Sport
Sport

swimming — Schwimmen
ice-skating — Eislauf
volleyball — Volleyball
riding — Reiten
badminton — Badminton
tennis — Tennis
golf — Golf
gymnastics — Turnen
rowing — Rudern
ice hockey — Eishockey
surfing — Surfen
skating — Skaten

Billy's basics

I like	– ich mag	I don't like	– ich mag nicht
you like	– du magst	you don't like	– du magst nicht
he, she, it likes	– er, sie, es mag	he, she, it doesn't like	– er, sie, es mag nicht
we like	– wir mögen	we don't like	– wir mögen nicht
you like	– ihr mögt	you don't like	– ihr mögt nicht
they like	– sie mögen	they don't like	– sie mögen nicht

cross-country skiing
Skilanglauf

basketball
Basketball

jogging
Joggen

water-skiing
Wasserski

football / soccer
Fußball

sailing
Segeln

snowboarding
Snowboarden

bobsleighing
Bob fahren

weightlifting
Gewichtheben

dancing
Tanzen

downhill
Abfahrt (Ski)

cycling
Radsport

Make sentences!

I like volleyball.
Ich mag Volleyball.
She doesn't like tennis.
Sie mag kein Tennis.

Do you like surfing? Yes, I do.
Magst du surfen? Ja.
Do you like dancing? No, I don't.
Magst du Tanzen? Nein.

At the campsite
Auf dem Zeltplatz

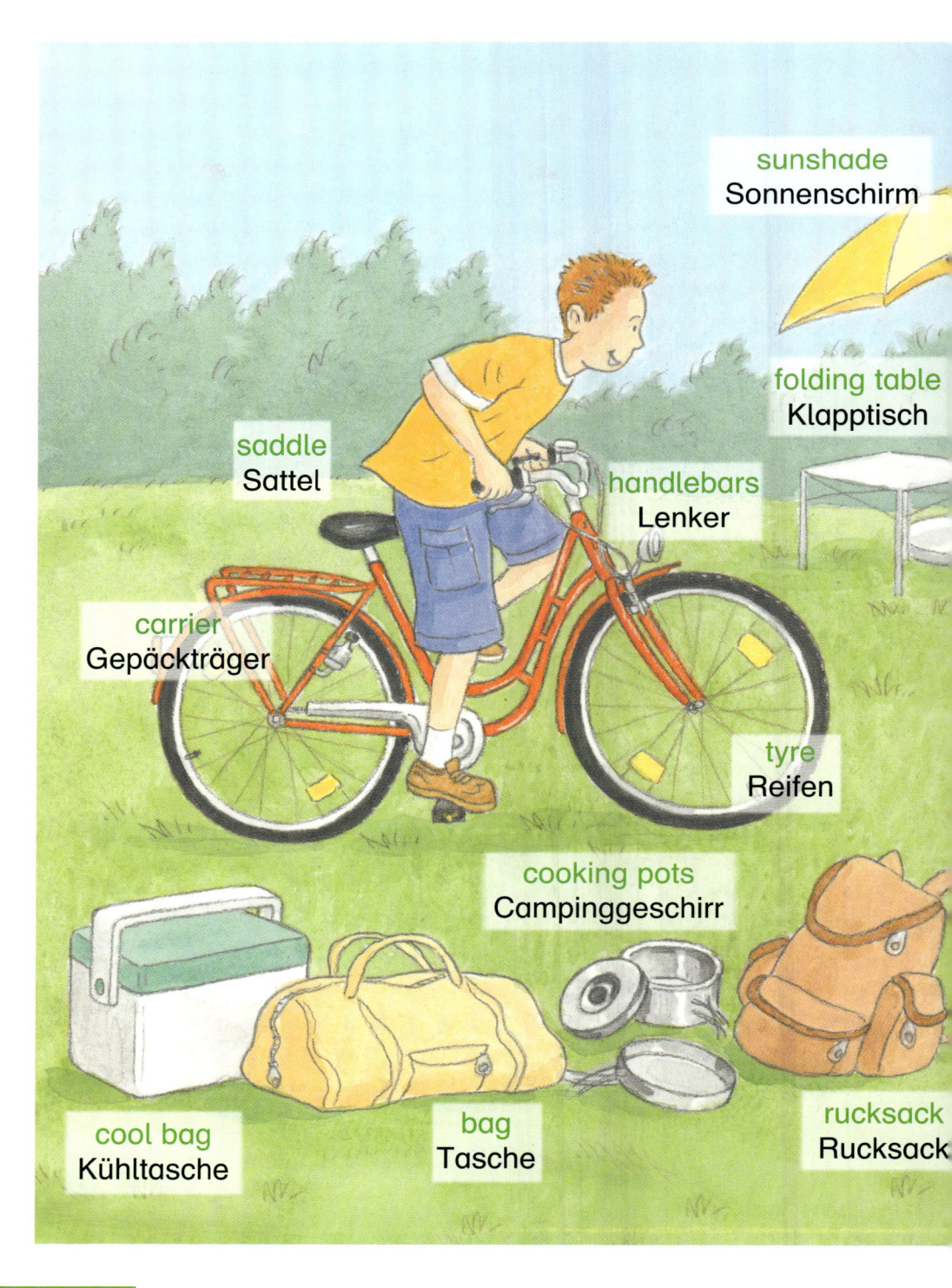

torch
Taschenlampe

camping stove
Gaskocher

thermos flask
Thermosflasche

cooking pots
Campinggeschirr

tins
Konserven

sunshade
Sonnenschirm

folding table
Klapptisch

saddle
Sattel

handlebars
Lenker

carrier
Gepäckträger

tyre
Reifen

cooking pots
Campinggeschirr

cool bag
Kühltasche

bag
Tasche

rucksack
Rucksack

Billy's basics

to give — geben
Give me..., please. — Gib mir..., bitte

tent	Zelt
folding chair	Klappstuhl
tent peg	Hering
rope	Leine
thermos flask	Thermosflasche
cushion	Kissen
air mattress	Luftmatratze
foam mattress	Isomatte
sleeping bag	Schlafsack
bellows	Blasebalg
tins	Konserven
torch	Taschenlampe
camping stove	Gaskocher
hiking boots	Wanderstiefel
candles	Kerzen
zip	Reißverschluss

Make sentences!

Give me the cushion, please.
Gib mir das Kissen, bitte.

Give me the torch, please.
Gib mir die Taschenlampe, bitte.

At the doctor's
Beim Arzt

gargle	Gurgelmittel
sore throat	Halsschmerzen
stomach ache	Bauchschmerzen
hot-water bottle	Wärmflasche
cold compress	kalte Kompresse
headache	Kopfschmerzen
cold	Schnupfen
handkerchief	Taschentuch
thermometer	Thermometer
fever	Fieber
sweaty feet	Schweißfüße
foot bath	Fußbad
cough medicine	Hustensaft
cough	Husten
flu	Grippe
tablets	Tabletten

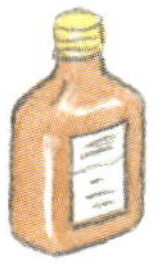

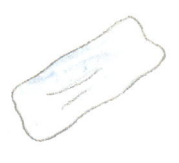

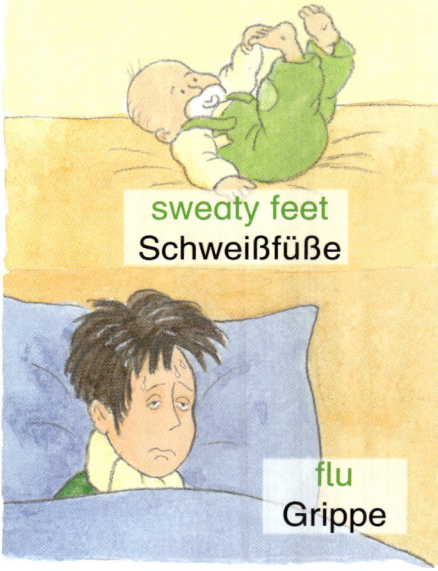

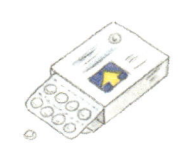

Billy's basics

I need – ich brauche
you need – du brauchst
he, she, it needs – er, sie, es braucht
we need – wir brauchen
you need – ihr braucht
they need – sie brauchen

plaster	Gips		plaster	Pflaster
		fracture — Knochenbruch		
		wound — Wunde		
glasses	Brille	can't see well — kann schlecht sehen	sprained arm — verstauchter Arm	bandage	Verband
hearing aid	Hörgerät	can't hear well — kann schlecht hören	spots — Pickel	ointment	Salbe
dentist	Zahnarzt	toothache — Zahnschmerzen	backache — Rückenschmerzen	injection	Spritze

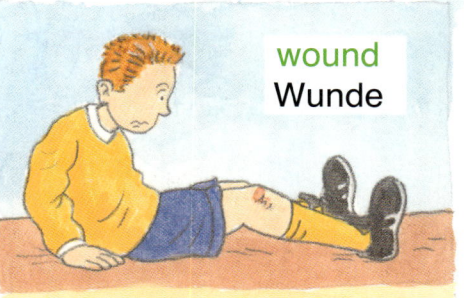

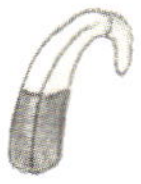

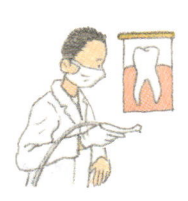

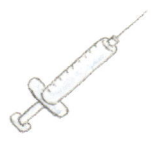

Make sentences!

Tom has a fracture. He needs a plaster.
Tom hat einen Knochenbruch. Er braucht einen Gips.

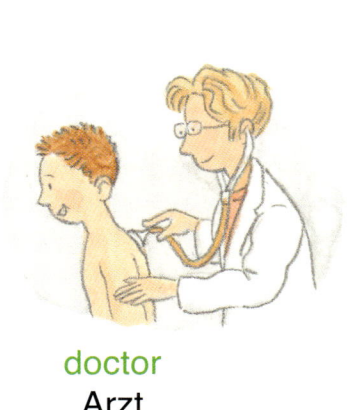

Professions
Berufe

doctor
Arzt

baker
Bäcker

hairdresser
Friseur

computer programmer
Programmierer

dentist
Zahnarzt

astronaut
Astronaut

policeman
Polizist

singer
Sängerin

painter and decorator
Maler und Anstreicher

chef
Koch

Billy's basics

When I'm older... — Wenn ich älter bin...
When I'm grown up... — Wenn ich erwachsen bin...
I want to be... — Ich will... werden.

teacher
Lehrerin

butcher
Fleischer

farmer
Bauer

dancer
Tänzer

fireman
Feuerwehrmann

tailor
Schneider

postman
Postbote

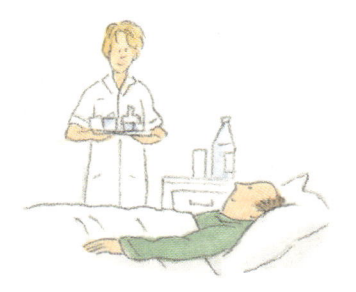

nurse
Krankenschwester

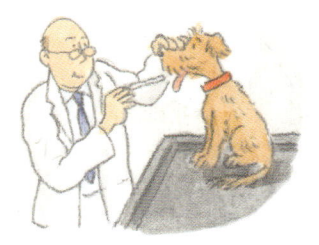

manager
Manager

vet
Tierarzt

Make sentences!

When I'm older,
I want to be a singer.
Wenn ich älter bin,
will ich Sänger werden.

When I'm grown up,
I want to be a teacher.
Wenn ich erwachsen bin,
will ich Lehrer werden.

The weather
Das Wetter

| sunny | windy |
| sonnig | windig |

| frosty | warm |
| frostig | warm |

| rainy | cloudy |
| regnerisch | bewölkt |

Billy's basics

rain	– Regen	cloud	– Wolke	It's raining.
snow	– Schnee	sky	– Himmel	Es regnet.
wind	– Wind	sun	– Sonne	It's snowing.
storm	– Sturm	thunder	– Donner	Es schneit.
fog	– Nebel	lightning	– Blitz	It's hailing.
hail	– Hagel	thunderstorm	– Gewitter	Es hagelt.

stormy / stürmisch	**foggy** / neblig
hot / heiß	**wet** / nass
cold / kalt	**snowy** / verschneit

Make sentences!

What's the weather like today?
Wie ist das Wetter heute?

It's foggy today.
Heute ist es neblig.

What's the weather like today?
Wie ist das Wetter heute?

It's hailing today.
Heute hagelt es.

The year and the seasons
Das Jahr und die Jahreszeiten

spring
Frühling

summer
Sommer

autumn
Herbst

winter
Winter

Billy's basics

January	– Januar	May	– Mai	September	– September
February	– Februar	June	– Juni	October	– Oktober
March	– März	July	– Juli	November	– November
April	– April	August	– August	December	– Dezember

to eat ice cream Eis essen	**to build a snowman** einen Schneemann bauen	**to pick apples** Äpfel pflücken
to get a Christmas present ein Weihnachtsgeschenk bekommen	**to collect conkers** Kastanien sammeln	**to look for Easter eggs** Ostereier suchen
to fly a kite einen Drachen steigen lassen	**to swim in the lake** im See schwimmen	**to look at the first flowers** die ersten Blumen betrachten

Make sentences!

In January Billy builds a snowman.
Im Januar baut Billy einen Schneemann.

In summer Sally swims in the lake.
Im Sommer schwimmt Sally im See.

Vocabulary
Vokabeln

A
a [ə]	ein, eine	
ache [eɪk]	Schmerz	
adult ['ædʌlt]	Erwachsener	
air mattress ['eə,mætrəs]	Luftmatratze	
alphabet ['ælfəbet]	Alphabet	
ambulance ['æmbjʊləns]	Krankenwagen	
animal ['ænɪməl]	Tier	
ankle ['æŋkl]	Fußgelenk	
ant [ænt]	Ameise	
apple ['æpl]	Apfel	
apple tree ['æpl,triː]	Apfelbaum	
April ['eɪprəl]	April	
arm [ɑːm]	Arm	
armchair ['ɑːmtʃeə]	Sessel	
art [ɑːt]	Kunst	
astronaut ['æstrənɔːt]	Astronaut, Astronautin	
at home [ət 'həʊm]	zu Hause	
August ['ɔːgəst]	August	
aunt [ɑːnt]	Tante	
autumn ['ɔːtəm]	Herbst	

B
- baby, babies ['beɪbi] — Baby, Babys
- back [bæk] — Rücken
- backache ['bækeɪk] — Rückenschmerzen
- back bend ['bæk,bend] — Brücke (Gymnastik)
- backward roll ['bækwəd ,rəʊl] — Rolle rückwärts
- badminton ['bædmɪntən] — Badminton
- bag [bæg] — Tasche
- to bake [beɪk] — backen
- baker ['beɪkə] — Bäcker, Bäckerin
- balcony ['bælkəni] — Balkon
- ball [bɔːl] — Ball
- balloon [bəl'uːn] — Ballon
- banana [bə'nɑːnə] — Banane
- bandage ['bændɪdʒ] — Verband
- bank [bæŋk] — Bank
- barn [bɑːn] — Scheune
- basics ['beɪsɪks] — Grundlagen
- basin ['beɪsn] — Waschbecken
- basketball ['bɑːskɪtbɔːl] — Basketball
- bath [bɑːθ] — Badewanne
- bathmat ['bɑːθmæt] — Badematte
- bathrobe ['bɑːθrəʊb] — Bademantel
- bathroom ['bɑːθrʊm] — Badezimmer
- beach ball ['biːtʃ,bɔːl] — Wasserball
- bean [biːn] — Bohne
- bear [beə] — Bär
- beautiful ['bjuːtɪfʊl] — schön
- beaver ['biːvə] — Biber
- bed [bed] — Bett
- bee [biː] — Biene
- beetle ['biːtl] — Käfer
- behind [bɪ'haɪnd] — hinter
- bellows ['beləʊz] — Blasebalg
- belt [belt] — Gürtel
- bench [bentʃ] — Bank
- between [bɪ'twiːn] — zwischen
- bicycle ['baɪsɪkl] — Fahrrad
- big [bɪg] — groß
- big wheel [,bɪg'wiːl] — Riesenrad
- bikini [bɪ'kiːni] — Bikini
- bird [bɜːd] — Vogel
- biro ['baɪərəʊ] — Kugelschreiber
- biscuit ['bɪskɪt] — Keks
- black [blæk] — schwarz
- blackboard ['blækbɔːd] — Tafel
- blanket ['blæŋkɪt] — Decke
- blind [blaɪnd] — Rollo
- blouse [blaʊz] — Bluse
- blue [bluː] — blau
- boat [bəʊt] — Boot
- bobsleighing ['bɒbsleɪɪŋ] — Bob fahren
- body ['bɒdi] — Körper
- book [bʊk] — Buch
- bookshelf ['bʊkʃelf] — Bücherregal
- bookshop ['bʊkʃɒp] — Buchhandlung
- boot [buːt] — Stiefel
- bottle ['bɒtl] — Flasche
- bottom ['bɒtəm] — Po
- bowl [bəʊl] — Schüssel
- boy [bɔɪ] — Junge
- bread [bred] — Brot
- break [breɪk] — Pause
- brick [brɪk] — Ziegelstein
- bridge [brɪdʒ] — Brücke
- broom [bruːm] — Besen
- brother ['brʌðə] — Bruder
- brown [braʊn] — braun
- to brush [brʌʃ] — putzen

to brush the teeth [ˌbrʌʃ ðə 'tiːθ]	Zähne putzen
bucket ['bʌkɪt]	Eimer
budgie ['bʌdʒi]	Wellensittich
to build [bɪld]	bauen
bumper car ['bʌmpəˌkɑː]	Autoskooter
bus [bʌs]	Bus
bus stop ['bʌsˌstɒp]	Bushaltestelle
bush [bʊʃ]	Busch
busy ['bɪzi]	beschäftigt
but [bʌt]	aber
butcher ['bʊtʃə]	Metzger, Metzgerin
butter ['bʌtə]	Butter
butterfly, butterflies ['bʌtəflaɪ]	Schmetterling, Schmetterlinge

C

cage [keɪdʒ]	Käfig
cake [keɪk]	Kuchen
calendar ['kæləndə]	Kalender
to call [kɔːl]	rufen
campsite ['kæmpsaɪt]	Zeltplatz
camping stove ['kæmpɪŋ ˌstəʊv]	Gaskocher
can [kæn]	können
candle ['kændl]	Kerze
candy floss ['kændiflɒs]	Zuckerwatte
cap [kæp]	Mütze, Kappe
car [kɑː]	Auto
cardigan ['kɑːdɪgən]	Strickjacke
carpet ['kɑːpɪt]	Teppich
carrier ['kærɪə]	Gepäckträger
carrot ['kærət]	Karotte
to carry ['kæri]	tragen
cartwheel ['kɑːtwiːl]	Rad (Gymnastik)
cat [kæt]	Katze
cauliflower ['kɒlɪflaʊə]	Blumenkohl
CD [ˌsiːˈdiː]	CD
CD player [ˌsiːˈdiː ˌpleɪə]	CD-Spieler
chalk [tʃɔːk]	Kreide
chair [tʃeə]	Stuhl
cheek [tʃiːk]	Wange
cheese [tʃiːz]	Käse
chef [ʃef]	Koch, Köchin (Restaurant)
cherry, cherries ['tʃeri]	Kirsche, Kirschen
chest [tʃest]	Brust
chestnut ['tʃesnʌt]	Kastanie (Baum)
chewing gum ['tʃuːɪŋˌgʌm]	Kaugummi
chick [tʃɪk]	Küken
child, children [tʃaɪld], ['tʃɪldrən]	Kind, Kinder
children's room ['tʃɪldrənzˌruːm]	Kinderzimmer
chimney ['tʃɪmni]	Schornstein
chin [tʃɪn]	Kinn
chips [tʃɪps]	Pommes frites
chocolate ['tʃɒklət]	Schokolade
Christmas present ['krɪsməsˌpreznt]	Weihnachtsgeschenk
church [tʃɜːtʃ]	Kirche
to clean [tuː kliːn]	putzen
to climb [tuː klaɪm]	klettern
clock [klɒk]	Uhr
closed [kləʊzd]	geschlossen
clothes [kləʊðz]	Kleidung
cloud [klaʊd]	Wolke
cloudy ['klaʊdi]	bewölkt
clown [klaʊn]	Clown
coat [kəʊt]	Mantel
cock [kɒk]	Hahn
cocoa ['kəʊkəʊ]	Kakao
coffee ['kɒfi]	Kaffee
coffee machine ['kɒfi məˌʃiːn]	Kaffeemaschine
coke [kəʊk]	Cola
cold [kəʊld]	kalt
cold [kəʊld]	Schnupfen
cold compress [kəʊld 'kɒmpres]	kalte Kompresse
to collect [kə'lekt]	sammeln
colour ['kʌlə]	Farbe
comb [kəʊm]	Kamm
combine harvester [ˌkɒmbaɪn 'hɑːvɪstə]	Mähdrescher
computer [kəm'pjuːtə]	Computer
conker ['kɒŋkə]	Kastanie (Frucht)
cook [kʊk]	Koch, Köchin
cooker ['kʊkə]	Herd
cooking pots ['kʊkɪŋˌpɒts]	Campinggeschirr
cool bag ['kuːlbæg]	Kühltasche

cough [kɒf]	Husten	dustbin ['dʌstbɪn]	Mülleimer
cough medicine ['kɒf ˌmedsɪn]	Hustensaft	dustpan ['dʌstpæn]	Kehrblech
cousin ['kʌzn]	Cousine, Cousin	**E** eagle ['i:gl]	Adler
cow [kaʊ]	Kuh	ear [ɪə]	Ohr
crocodile ['krɒkədaɪl]	Krokodil	Easter egg ['i:stəˌeg]	Osterei
cross-country skiing [ˌkrɒskʌntri 'ski:ɪŋ]	Skilanglauf	to eat [i:t]	essen
to cry [kraɪ]	weinen	egg [eg]	Ei
cucumber ['kju:kʌmbə]	Gurke	elbow ['elbəʊ]	Ellbogen
cup [kʌp]	Tasse	elephant ['elɪfənt]	Elefant
cupboard ['kʌbəd]	Schrank	empty ['empti]	leer
cushion ['kʊʃən]	Kissen	exercise book ['eksəsaɪzˌbʊk]	Heft
cycling ['saɪklɪŋ]	Radsport	eye [aɪ]	Auge
D to dance [dɑ:ns]	tanzen	eyebrow ['aɪbraʊ]	Augenbraue
dancer ['dɑ:nsə]	Tänzer, Tänzerin	**F** fair [feə]	Jahrmarkt
dancing ['dɑ:nsɪŋ]	Tanzen	family ['fæmɪli]	Familie
daughter ['dɔ:tə]	Tochter	farm [fɑ:m]	Bauernhof
December [dɪ'sembə]	Dezember	farmer ['fɑ:mə]	Bauer
dentist ['dentɪst]	Zahnarzt, Zahnärztin	farmer's wife [ˌfɑ:məz 'waɪf]	Bäuerin
desk [desk]	Schreibtisch, Pult	farmhouse ['fɑ:mhaʊs]	Bauernhaus
dishcloth ['dɪʃklɒθ]	Geschirrtuch	farmyard ['fɑ:mjɑ:d]	Hof
dishes ['dɪʃɪz]	Geschirr	fast [fɑ:st]	schnell
dishwasher ['dɪʃˌwɒʃə]	Spülmaschine	fat [fæt]	dick
to dive [daɪv]	tauchen	father ['fɑ:ðə]	Vater
diving board ['daɪvɪŋˌbɔ:d]	Sprungbrett	feather ['feðə]	Feder
diving ring ['daɪvɪŋˌrɪŋ]	Tauchring	February ['februəri]	Februar
to do [du:]	tun, machen	fence [fens]	Zaun
to do homework [ˌdu: 'həʊmwɜ:k]	Hausaufgaben machen	fever ['fi:və]	Fieber
doctor ['dɒktə]	Arzt, Ärztin	field [fi:ld]	Feld
dog [dɒg]	Hund	finger ['fɪŋgə]	Finger
dog bowl ['dɒgˌbəʊl]	Hundenapf	fire engine ['faɪəˌrendʒɪn]	Feuerwehrauto
doll [dɒl]	Puppe	fireman ['faɪəmən]	Feuerwehrmann
dolphin ['dɒlfɪn]	Delfin	firewoman ['faɪəˌwʊmən]	Feuerwehrfrau
door [dɔ:]	Tür	fish [fɪʃ]	Fisch, Fische
downhill ['daʊnhɪl]	Abfahrt (Ski)	flamingo [flə'mɪŋgəʊ]	Flamingo
dragon ['drægən]	Drachen	floor [flɔ:]	Fußboden
to draw [drɔ:]	zeichnen	flower ['flaʊə]	Blume
drawer [drɔ:]	Schublade	flu [flu:]	Grippe
to dream [dri:m]	träumen	flush [flʌʃ]	Spülung (Toilette)
dress [dres]	Kleid	to fly [flaɪ]	fliegen
to drink [drɪŋk]	trinken	fly, flies [flaɪ]	Fliege, Fliegen
duck [dʌk]	Ente	foam mattress ['fəʊmˌmætrəs]	Isomatte
dunghill ['dʌŋhɪl]	Misthaufen	fog [fɒg]	Nebel
		foggy ['fɒgi]	neblig

folding chair	[ˌfəʊldɪŋ 'tʃeə]	Klappstuhl	
folding table	[ˌfəʊldɪŋ 'teɪbl]	Klapptisch	
food	[fuːd]	das Lebensmittel, die Lebensmittel	
foot, feet	[fʊt], [fiːt]	Fuß, Füße	
foot bath	['fʊtbɑːθ]	Fußbad	
football	['fʊtbɔːl]	Fußball	
forehead	['fɔːhed]	Stirn	
fork	[fɔːk]	Gabel	
forward roll	['fɔːwəd ˌrəʊl]	Rolle vorwärts	
fox	[fɒks]	Fuchs	
fracture	['fræktʃə]	Knochenbruch	
Friday	['fraɪdeɪ]	Freitag	
fridge	[frɪdʒ]	Kühlschrank	
frosty	['frɒsti]	frostig	
fruit	[fruːt]	Obst	
full	[fʊl]	voll	

G

garage	['gærɑːʒ, 'gærɪdʒ]	Garage
garden	['gɑːdn]	Garten
gargle	['gɑːgl]	Gurgelmittel
gate	[geɪt]	Tor
to get older	[ˌget 'əʊldə]	älter werden
ghost train	['gəʊstˌtreɪn]	Geisterbahn
giraffe	[dʒɪ'rɑːf]	Giraffe
girl	[gɜːl]	Mädchen
to give	[gɪv]	geben
glass	[glɑːs]	Glas
glasses	['glɑːsɪz]	Brille
glove	[glʌv]	Handschuh
to go	[gəʊ]	gehen
to go for a walk	[ˌgəʊ fər ə 'wɔːk]	spazieren gehen
to go shopping	[ˌgəʊ 'ʃɒpɪŋ]	einkaufen gehen
goat	[gəʊt]	Ziege
golf	[gɒlf]	Golf
grandchild	['grændtʃaɪld]	Enkelkind
grandchildren	['grændtʃɪldrən]	Enkelkinder
grandfather	['grændfɑːðə]	Großvater
grandmother	['grændmʌðə]	Großmutter
grape	[greɪp]	Weintraube
grass	[grɑːs]	Gras
green	[griːn]	grün
grey	[greɪ]	grau
to grow up	[ˌgrəʊ 'ʌp]	erwachsen werden
guinea pig	['gɪni pɪg]	Meerschweinchen
gutter	['gʌtə]	Dachrinne
gymnastics	[dʒɪm'næstɪks]	Turnen

H

hail	[heɪl]	Hagel
to hail	[heɪl]	hageln
hair	[heə]	Haar
hairbrush	['heəbrʌʃ]	Haarbürste
hairdresser	['heəˌdresə]	Friseur, Friseurin
hair-dryer	['heəˌdraɪə]	Föhn
ham	[hæm]	Schinken
hamburger	['hæmˌbɜːgə]	Hamburger
hammer	['hæmə]	Hammer
hamster	['hæmstə]	Hamster
hand	[hænd]	Hand
handkerchief	['hæŋkətʃiːf]	Taschentuch
handlebars	['hændlbɑːz]	Lenker (Fahrrad)
handstand	['hændstænd]	Handstand
happy	['hæpi]	glücklich
hard	[hɑːd]	hart
hare	[heə]	Hase
hat	[hæt]	Hut
to have	[hæv]	haben
to have got	[hæv'gɒt]	haben
hay	[heɪ]	Heu
head	[hed]	Kopf
headache	['hedeɪk]	Kopfschmerzen
headstand	['hedstænd]	Kopfstand
to hear	[hɪə]	hören
hearing aid	['hɪərɪŋˌeɪd]	Hörgerät
hedge	[hedʒ]	Hecke
hedgehog	['hedʒhɒg]	Igel
helicopter	['helɪkɒptə]	Hubschrauber
hen	[hen]	Henne
henhouse	['henhaʊs]	Hühnerstall
high	[haɪ]	hoch
hiking boots	['haɪkɪŋ ˌbuːts]	Wanderschuhe
hippo	['hɪpəʊ]	Flusspferd
honey	['hʌni]	Honig
horse	[hɔːs]	Pferd
hospital	['hɒspɪtl]	Krankenhaus
hot	[hɒt]	heiß
hot dog	['hɒtdɒg]	Hotdog

hot-water bottle [ˌhɒtˈwɔːtəˌbɒtl]	Wärmflasche	letter boxes [ˈletəˌbɒkɪz]	Briefkästen
house [haʊs]	Haus	lettuce [ˈletɪs]	Salat
husband [ˈhʌzbənd]	Ehemann	life belt [ˈlaɪfbelt]	Rettungsring

I ice cream [ˌaɪsˈkriːm] — Eis
ice hockey [ˌaɪsˈhɒki] — Eishockey
ice-skating [ˈaɪsˌskeɪtɪŋ] — Eislauf
in front of [ɪn ˈfrʌnt əv] — vor
indicator [ˈɪndɪkeɪtə] — Anzeige
injection [ɪnˈdʒekʃən] — Spritze
iron [ˈaɪən] — Bügeleisen
ironing board [ˈaɪənɪŋˌbɔːd] — Bügelbrett
ivy [ˈaɪvi] — Efeu

J jacket [ˈdʒækɪt] — Jacke
jam [dʒæm] — Marmelade
January [ˈdʒænuəri] — Januar
jeans [dʒiːnz] — Jeans
jogging [ˈdʒɒgɪŋ] — Joggen
July [dʒuˈlaɪ] — Juli
to jump [dʒʌmp] — springen
jumper [ˈdʒʌmpə] — Pullover
June [dʒuːn] — Juni

K kangaroo [ˌkæŋgəˈruː] — Känguru
kennel [ˈkenl] — Hundehütte
to kiss [kɪs] — küssen
kitchen [ˈkɪtʃɪn] — Küche
kite [kaɪt] — Drachen
knee [niː] — Knie
knee bend [ˈniːbend] — Kniebeuge
knife [naɪf] — Messer
to knock [nɒk] — klopfen
to know [nəʊ] — wissen, kennen

L ladder [ˈlædə] — Leiter
ladybird [ˈleɪdibɜːd] — Marienkäfer
lake [leɪk] — See
lamp [læmp] — Lampe
to laugh [lɑːf] — lachen
lawn [lɔːn] — Rasen
leaf, leaves [liːf] — Blatt, Blätter
left [left] — links
leg [leg] — Bein
lemon [ˈlemən] — Zitrone
lemonade [ˌleməˈneɪd] — Limonade
lesson [ˈlesən] — Unterrichtsstunde
letter box [ˈletəˌbɒks] — Briefkasten

lightning [ˈlaɪtnɪŋ] — Blitz
to like [laɪk] — mögen
lilo [ˈlaɪləʊ] — Luftmatratze
lion [ˈlaɪən] — Löwe
to listen [ˈlɪsn] — zuhören
living room [ˈlɪvɪŋrʊm] — Wohnzimmer
long [lɒŋ] — lang
to look [lʊk] — schauen
to look for [ˈlʊk fɔː] — suchen
loud [laʊd] — laut
lorry [ˈlɒri] — LKW
loudspeaker [ˌlaʊdˈspiːkə] — Lautsprecher
low [ləʊ] — niedrig
lunch [lʌntʃ] — Mittagessen

M magazine [ˌmægəˈziːn] — Zeitschrift
to make [meɪk] — machen
man [mæn] — Mann
manager [ˈmænɪdʒə] — Manager
map [mæp] — Landkarte
March [mɑːtʃ] — März
May [meɪ] — Mai
microwave [ˈmaɪkrəʊweɪv] — Mikrowelle
milk [mɪlk] — Milch
mirror [ˈmɪrə] — Spiegel
mittens [ˈmɪtnz] — Fäustlinge
mobile phone [ˌməʊbaɪl ˈfəʊn] — Handy
Monday [ˈmʌndeɪ] — Montag
monkey [ˈmʌŋki] — Affe
mother [ˈmʌðə] — Mutter
motorbike [ˈməʊtəbaɪk] — Motorrad
mouse [maʊs] — Maus
mouth [maʊθ] — Mund
museum [mjuːˈziːəm] — Museum
mushrooms [ˈmʌʃrʊmz] — Pilze

N neck [nek] — Hals
to need [niːd] — brauchen
newspaper [ˈnjuːzˌpeɪpə] — Zeitung
next to [ˈnekst tuː] — neben
nightdress [ˈnaɪtdres] — Nachthemd
nose [nəʊz] — Nase

November [nəʊ'vembə]	November	pillow ['pɪləʊ]	Kopfkissen
number ['nʌmbə]	Zahl, Nummer	pineapple ['paɪnæpl]	Ananas
nurse [nɜːs]	Krankenschwester	pink [pɪŋk]	rosa
October [ɒk'təʊbə]	Oktober	pitchfork ['pɪtʃfɔːk]	Mistgabel
oil [ɔɪl]	Öl	plant [plɑːnt]	Pflanze
ointment ['ɔɪntmənt]	Salbe	plaster ['plɑːstə]	Gips, Pflaster
old [əʊld]	alt	plastic flower [ˌplæstɪk'flaʊə]	Plastikblume
on [ɒn]	auf	plate [pleɪt]	Teller
one-leg stand [ˌwʌnleg 'stænd]	Waage (Sport)	to play [pleɪ]	spielen
open ['əʊpən]	geöffnet	playpen ['pleɪpen]	Laufstall
opposite ['ɒpəzɪt]	Gegenteil, Gegensatz	please [pliːz]	bitte
orange ['ɒrɪndʒ]	Orange, orange	plum [plʌm]	Pflaume
orange juice ['ɒrɪndʒˌdʒuːs]	Orangensaft	polar bear ['pəʊləˌbeə]	Eisbär
oven [ʌvn]	Backofen	police car [pə'liːsˌkɑː]	Polizeiauto
oven cloth ['ʌvnklɒθ]	Topflappen	policeman [pə'liːsmən]	Polizist
over ['əʊvə]	über	policewoman [pə'liːsˌwʊmən]	Polizistin
to paint [peɪnt]	malen	pond [pɒnd]	Teich
painter and decorator ['peɪntər ənd 'dekəreɪtə]	Maler(in) und Anstreicher(in)	pool [puːl]	Becken
pan [pæn]	Pfanne	popcorn ['pɒpkɔːn]	Popcorn
pants [pænts]	Unterhose	post office ['pəʊstˌɒfɪs]	Postamt
paper ['peɪpə]	Papier	poster ['pəʊstə]	Poster
parents ['peərənts]	Eltern	postman ['pəʊstmən]	Postbote
parrot ['pærət]	Papagei	pot [pɒt]	Topf
part [pɑːt]	Teil	potato, potatoes [pə'teɪtəʊ], [pə'teɪtəʊz]	Kartoffel, Kartoffeln
pasture ['pɑːstʃə]	Weide	pound [paʊnd]	Pfund
pavement ['peɪvmənt]	Bürgersteig	profession [prə'feʃən]	Beruf
peach [piːtʃ]	Pfirsich	programmer ['prəʊgræmə]	Programmierer
peacock ['piːkɒk]	Pfau	pub [pʌb]	Kneipe
pear [peə]	Birne	to pull [pʊl]	ziehen
peas [piːz]	Erbsen	pupil ['pjuːpl]	Schüler
pen [pen]	Füller	puppet ['pʌpɪt]	Handpuppe
pencil ['pensl]	Bleistift	puppet theatre ['pʌpɪtˌθɪətə]	Puppentheater
pencil case ['penslˌkeɪs]	Mäppchen	purple ['pɜːpl]	lila
pencil sharpener ['penslˌʃɑːpnə]	Anspitzer	to push [pʊʃ]	drücken
penguin ['peŋgwɪn]	Pinguin	pyjamas [pɪ'dʒɑːməz]	Schlafanzug
pepper ['pepə]	Pfeffer	**quiet** ['kwaɪət]	leise
petrol station ['petrəlˌsteɪʃn]	Tankstelle	**rabbit** ['ræbɪt]	Kaninchen
to pick [pɪk]	pflücken	radiator ['reɪdieɪtə]	Heizung
picture ['pɪktʃə]	Bild	radio ['reɪdiəʊ]	Radio
picture book ['pɪktʃəˌbʊk]	Bilderbuch	rain [reɪn]	Regen
pig [pɪg]	Schwein	to rain [reɪn]	regnen

raincoat ['reɪnkəʊt]	Regenmantel	season ['siːzn]	Jahreszeit
rainy ['reɪni]	regnerisch	to see [siː]	sehen
to read [riːd]	lesen	seesaw ['siːsɔː]	Wippe
red [red]	rot	sentence ['sentəns]	Satz
red pepper [ˌred 'pepə]	roter Paprika	September [sep'tembə]	September
remote control [rɪˌməʊt kən'trəʊl]	Fernbedienung	sheep [ʃiːp]	Schaf, Schafe
		shoes [ʃuːz]	Schuhe
rhino ['raɪnəʊ]	Nashorn	shop [ʃɒp]	Geschäft
riding ['raɪdɪŋ]	Reiten	shopping centre ['ʃɒpɪŋˌsentə]	Einkaufszentrum
right [raɪt]	rechts, richtig		
ring [rɪŋ]	Ring	short [ʃɔːt]	kurz
river ['rɪvə]	Fluss	shorts [ʃɔːts]	Shorts
roller coaster ['rəʊləˌkəʊstə]	Achterbahn	shoulder ['ʃəʊldə]	Schulter
		to shout [ʃaʊt]	rufen
roof [ruːf]	Dach	to show [ʃəʊ]	zeigen
rope [rəʊp]	Leine, Seil	shower ['ʃaʊə]	Dusche
rose [rəʊz]	Rose	shower curtain ['ʃaʊəˌkɜːtn]	Duschvorhang
roundabout ['raʊndəˌbaʊt]	Karussell		
to row [rəʊ]	rudern	shower gel ['ʃaʊəˌdʒel]	Duschgel
rowing ['rəʊɪŋ]	Rudern		
rubber ['rʌbə]	Gummi, Radiergummi	to sing [sɪŋ]	singen
rubber boot ['rʌbəˌbuːt]	Gummistiefel	singer ['sɪŋə]	Sänger, Sängerin
rubber duck ['rʌbəˌdʌk]	Gummiente	sink [sɪŋk]	Spüle
rubber ring ['rʌbəˌrɪŋ]	Schwimmring	sister ['sɪstə]	Schwester
rubbish bin ['rʌbɪʃˌbɪn]	Mülleimer	to sit [sɪt]	sitzen
rucksack ['rʌksæk]	Rucksack	skating ['skeɪtɪŋ]	Skaten
ruler ['ruːlə]	Lineal	skiing ['skiːɪŋ]	Ski fahren
to run [rʌn]	rennen	skipping rope ['skɪpɪŋˌrəʊp]	Hüpfseil
S sad [sæd]	traurig		
saddle ['sædl]	Sattel	skirt [skɜːt]	Rock
sailing ['seɪlɪŋ]	Segeln	sky [skaɪ]	Himmel
salt [sɔːlt]	Salz	to sleep [sliːp]	schlafen
sand [sænd]	Sand	sleeping bag ['sliːpɪŋˌbæg]	Schlafsack
sandals ['sændlz]	Sandalen	slide [slaɪd]	Rutsche
sandpit ['sændpɪt]	Sandkasten	slippers ['slɪpəz]	Hausschuhe
satchel ['sætʃl]	Schultasche	slow [sləʊ]	langsam
saucer ['sɔːsə]	Untertasse	small [smɔːl]	klein
sauna ['sɔːnə]	Sauna	to smile [smaɪl]	lächeln
sausage ['sɒsɪdʒ]	Würstchen	snake [sneɪk]	Schlange
saxophone ['sæksəfəʊn]	Saxophon	snow [snəʊ]	Schnee
scarf [skɑːf]	Schal	to snow [snəʊ]	schneien
school [skuːl]	Schule	snowboarding ['snəʊbɔːdɪŋ]	Snowboarden
school uniform [ˌskuːl 'juːnɪfɔːm]	Schuluniform		
		snowman ['snəʊmæn]	Schneemann
scissors ['sɪzəz]	Schere, Scheren	snowy ['snəʊi]	verschneit

soap [səʊp]	Seife	swimming pool ['swɪmɪŋˌpuːl]	Schwimmbad
soccer ['sɑkə]	Fußball	swimming trunks ['swɪmɪŋˌtrʌŋks]	Badehose
socket ['sɒkɪt]	Steckdose	swimsuit ['swɪmsuːt]	Badeanzug
socks [sɒks]	Socken	to swing [swɪŋ]	schaukeln
sofa ['səʊfə]	Sofa	**T table** ['teɪbl]	Tisch
soft [sɒft]	weich	tablet ['tæblɪt]	Tablette
solarium [səʊ'leərɪəm]	Solarium	tailor ['teɪlə]	Schneider, Schneiderin
son [sʌn]	Sohn		
sore throat [ˌsɔː 'θrəʊt]	Halsschmerzen	to take [teɪk]	nehmen
spade [speɪd]	Schaufel, Schippe	to talk [tɔːk]	reden
spider ['spaɪdə]	Spinne	tap [tæp]	Wasserhahn
spider's web ['spaɪdəzˌweb]	Spinnennetz	tea [tiː]	Tee
sponge [spʌndʒ]	Schwamm	teacher ['tiːtʃə]	Lehrer, Lehrerin
spoon [spuːn]	Löffel	teddy bear ['tediˌbeə]	Teddybär
sport [spɔːt]	Sport	telephone ['telɪfəʊn]	Telefon
spots [spɒts]	Pickel	television ['telɪvɪʒən]	Fernsehen
to sprain [spreɪn]	verstauchen	temperature ['temprɪtʃə]	Temperatur
spring [sprɪŋ]	Frühling		
squirrel ['skwɪrəl]	Eichhörnchen	tennis ['tenɪs]	Tennis
stable ['steɪbl]	Stall	tent [tent]	Zelt
stairs [steəz]	Treppe, Stufen	tent peg ['tentpeg]	Hering (Zelt)
starting block ['staːtɪŋˌblɒk]	Startblock	thank you ['θæŋkju]	danke
stomach ['stʌmək]	Bauch, Magen	there [ðeə]	dort
stomach ache ['stʌməkˌeɪk]	Bauchschmerzen	thermometer [θə'mɒmɪtə]	Thermometer
		thermos flask ['θɜːmɒs flɑːsk]	Thermoskanne
stone [stəʊn]	Stein		
storm [stɔːm]	Sturm	thin [θɪn]	dünn
stormy ['stɔːmi]	stürmisch	thing [θɪŋ]	Sache, Ding
straw [strɔː]	Stroh	to think [θɪŋk]	denken
strawberry ['strɔːbəri]	Erdbeere	thumb [θʌm]	Daumen
sugar ['ʃʊgə]	Zucker	thunder ['θʌndə]	Donner
suit [suːt]	Anzug	thunderstorm ['θʌndəˌstɔːm]	Gewitter
summer ['sʌmə]	Sommer		
sun [sʌn]	Sonne	Thursday ['θɜːzdeɪ]	Donnerstag
sun lounger ['sʌnˌlaʊndʒə]	Sonnenliege	ticket ['tɪkɪt]	Los, Eintrittskarte
sunflower ['sʌnflaʊə]	Sonnenblume	tie [taɪ]	Krawatte
sunny ['sʌni]	sonnig	tiger ['taɪgə]	Tiger
sunshade ['sʌnʃeɪd]	Sonnenschirm	tights [taɪts]	Strumpfhose
supermarket ['suːpəˌmaːkɪt]	Supermarkt	tile [taɪl]	Fliese
surfing ['sɜːfɪŋ]	Surfen	time [taɪm]	Zeit
sweetcorn ['swiːtkɔːn]	Mais	timetable ['taɪmˌteɪbl]	Stundenplan
to swim [swɪm]	schwimmen	tin [tɪn]	Konservendose
swimming ['swɪmɪŋ]	Schwimmen	toad [təʊd]	Kröte

today [tə'deɪ]	heute	
toe [təʊ]	Zeh	
toilet ['tɔɪlət]	Toilette	
toilet paper ['tɔɪlət,peɪpə]	Toilettenpapier	
tomato, tomatoes [tə'mɑːtəʊ]	Tomate, Tomaten	
tooth, teeth [tuːθ], [tiːθ]	Zahn, Zähne	
toothache ['tuːθeɪk]	Zahnschmerzen	
toothbrush ['tuːθbrʌʃ]	Zahnbürste	
toothpaste ['tuːθpeɪst]	Zahncreme	
torch [tɔːtʃ]	Taschenlampe	
towel [taʊəl]	Handtuch	
tower [taʊə]	Turm	
town [taʊn]	Stadt	
toy [tɔɪ]	Spielzeug	
toy car ['tɔɪ ˌkɑː]	Spielzeugauto	
tractor ['træktə]	Traktor	
traffic lights ['træfɪk,laɪts]	Ampel	
traffic sign ['træfɪk,saɪn]	Verkehrsschild	
trainers ['treɪnəz]	Turnschuhe	
tree [triː]	Baum	
trousers ['traʊzəz]	Hose	
Tuesday ['tjuːzdeɪ, 'tʃuːzdeɪ]	Dienstag	
turtle ['tɜːtl]	Schildkröte	
tyre ['taɪə]	Reifen	
U umbrella [ʌm'brelə]	Regenschirm	
uncle ['ʌŋkl]	Onkel	
under ['ʌndə]	unter	
V vase [vɑːz]	Vase	
very ['veri]	sehr	
vest [vest]	Unterhemd	
vinegar ['vɪnɪgə]	Essig	
vocabulary [vəʊ'kæbjʊləri]	Vokabeln	
volleyball ['vɒlibɔːl]	Volleyball	
W to wait [weɪt]	warten	
to walk [wɔːk]	gehen	
to want [wɒnt]	wollen, möchten	
wardrobe ['wɔːdrəʊb]	Schrank	
warm [wɔːm]	warm	
water ['wɔːtə]	Wasser	
watering can ['wɔːtərɪŋkæn]	Gießkanne	
water skiing ['wɔːtəsˌkiːɪŋ]	Wasserski	
water slide ['wɔːtəslaɪd]	Wasserrutsche	
water wings ['wɔːtəwɪŋz]	Schwimmflügel	
weather ['weðə]	Wetter	
Wednesday ['wenzdeɪ]	Mittwoch	
weightlifting ['weɪtˌlɪftɪŋ]	Gewichtheben	
wellington boots [ˌwelɪŋtən 'buːts]	Gummistiefel	
wet [wet]	nass	
what [wɒt]	was	
wheel [wiːl]	Rad	
wheelbarrow ['wiːlˌbærəʊ]	Schubkarre	
when [wen]	wenn	
where [weə]	wo	
to whisper ['wɪspə]	flüstern	
who [huː]	wer	
wife [waɪf]	Ehefrau	
wind [wɪnd]	Wind	
window ['wɪndəʊ]	Fenster	
windowsill ['wɪndəʊsɪl]	Fensterbank	
windy ['wɪndi]	windig	
winter ['wɪntə]	Winter	
wolf, wolves [wʊlf]	Wolf, Wölfe	
woman ['wʊmən]	Frau	
worm [wɜːm]	Wurm	
wound [waʊnd]	Wunde	
to write [raɪt]	schreiben	
Y year [jɪə]	Jahr	
yellow ['jeləʊ]	gelb	
young [jʌŋ]	jung	
Z zebra ['zebrə]	Zebra	
zip [zɪp]	Reißverschluss	